YOGA MUSIC
FOR UKULELE

ISBN 978-1-5400-3860-9

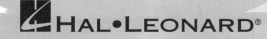

For all works contained herein:
Unauthorized copying, arranging, adapting, recording, Internet posting, public performance,
or other distribution of the music in this publication is an infringement of copyright.
Infringers are liable under the law.

Visit Hal Leonard Online at
www.halleonard.com

Contact us:
Hal Leonard
7777 West Bluemound Road
Milwaukee, WI 53213
Email: info@halleonard.com

In Europe, contact:
Hal Leonard Europe Limited
42 Wigmore Street
Marylebone, London, W1U 2RN
Email: info@halleonardeurope.com

In Australia, contact:
Hal Leonard Australia Pty. Ltd.
4 Lentara Court
Cheltenham, Victoria, 3192 Australia
Email: info@halleonard.com.au

Be Here Now

Words and Music by Ray LaMontagne

First note

1. Don't let your mind ___ get wea - ry and ___
2. Don't let your soul ___ get lone - ly, child. ___
3. Don't lose your faith ___ in me ___ and I ___

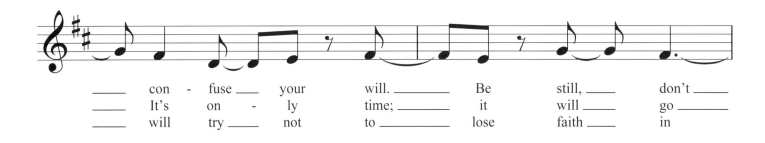

___ con - fuse ___ your will. ___ Be still, ___ don't ___
___ It's on - ly time; ___ it will ___ go ___
___ will try ___ not to ___ lose faith ___ in

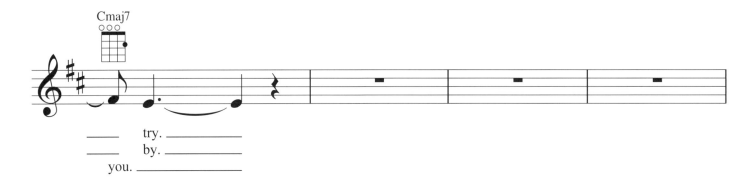

Cmaj7

___ try.
___ by.
you. ___

D

Don't let your heart ___ get heav - y, child. ___
Don't look for love ___ in fac - es, plac -
Don't put your trust ___ in walls ___ 'cause walls ___

Copyright © 2006 BMG Monarch and Sweet Mary Music
All Rights Administered by BMG Rights Management (US) LLC
All Rights Reserved   Used by Permission

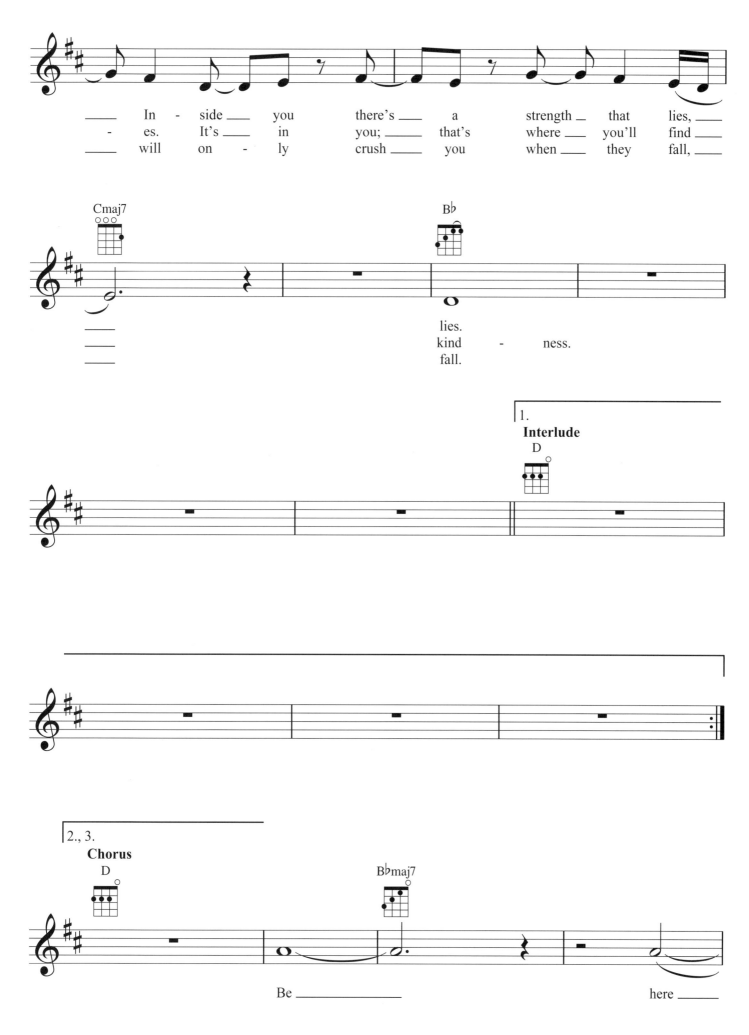

In - side ___ you there's ___ a strength ___ that lies, ___
\- es. It's ___ in you; ___ that's where ___ you'll find ___
___ will on - ly crush ___ you when ___ they fall, ___

Cmaj7   B♭

___ lies.
___ kind - ness.
___ fall.

1.
Interlude
D

2., 3.
Chorus
D   B♭maj7

Be ___   here ___

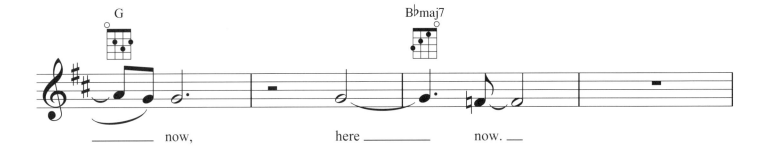

_____ now,   here _____   now. ___

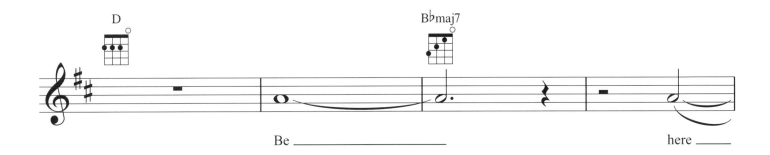

Be _____   here ___

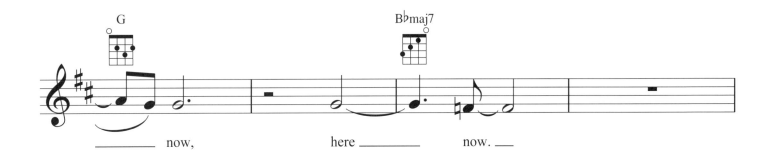

_____ now,   here _____   now. ___

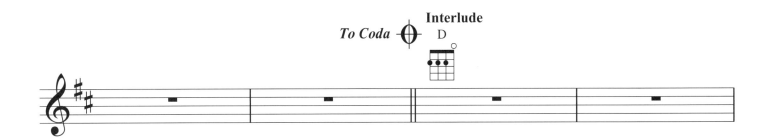

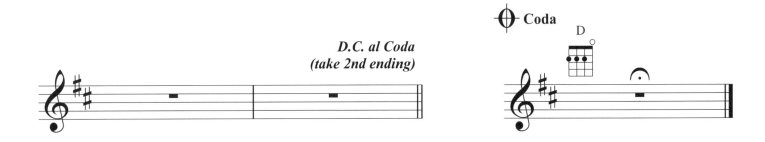

Angel

Words and Music by Jack Johnson

Copyright © 2007 by Sleep Through The Static Music (ASCAP)
All Rights Reserved   Used by Permission

with her pres - ence a - lone. _____

She gives me ev - 'ry-thing I could wish __ for; she gives me kiss -

- es on the lips just for com - ing _____ home.

Verse

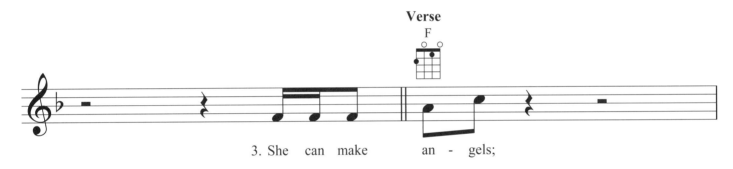

3. She can make an - gels;

seen it with my ___ own _____ eyes. _____

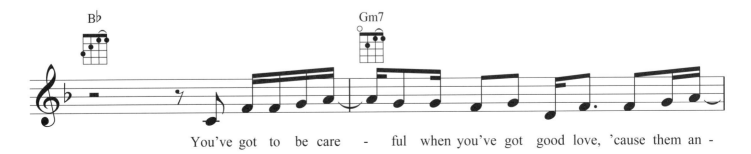

You've got to be care - ful when you've got good love, 'cause them an -

- gels will ___ just keep ___ on mul - ti - ply - ing.

Outro

But you're so bus - y chang-ing the world. ___ Just one smile ___

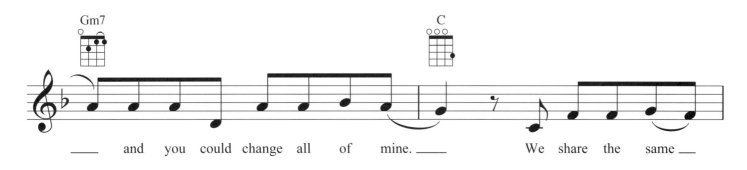

___ and you could change all of mine. ___ We share the same ___

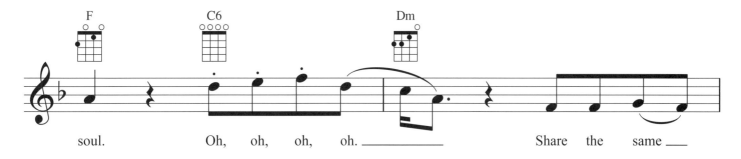

soul. Oh, oh, oh, oh. _____ Share the same ___

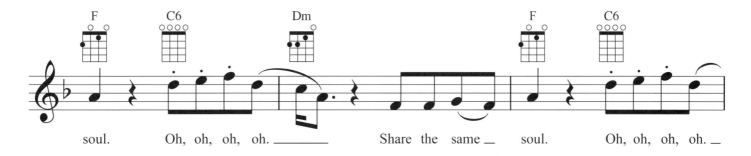

soul. Oh, oh, oh, oh. _____ Share the same ___ soul. Oh, oh, oh, oh. __

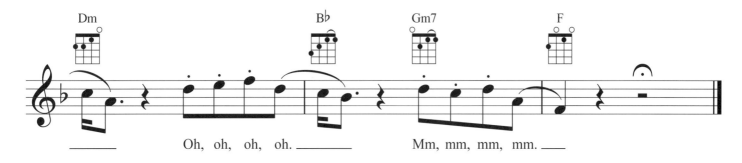

_____ Oh, oh, oh, oh. _____ Mm, mm, mm, mm. ___

Breathe Me

Words and Music by Dan Carey and Sia Kate I. Furler

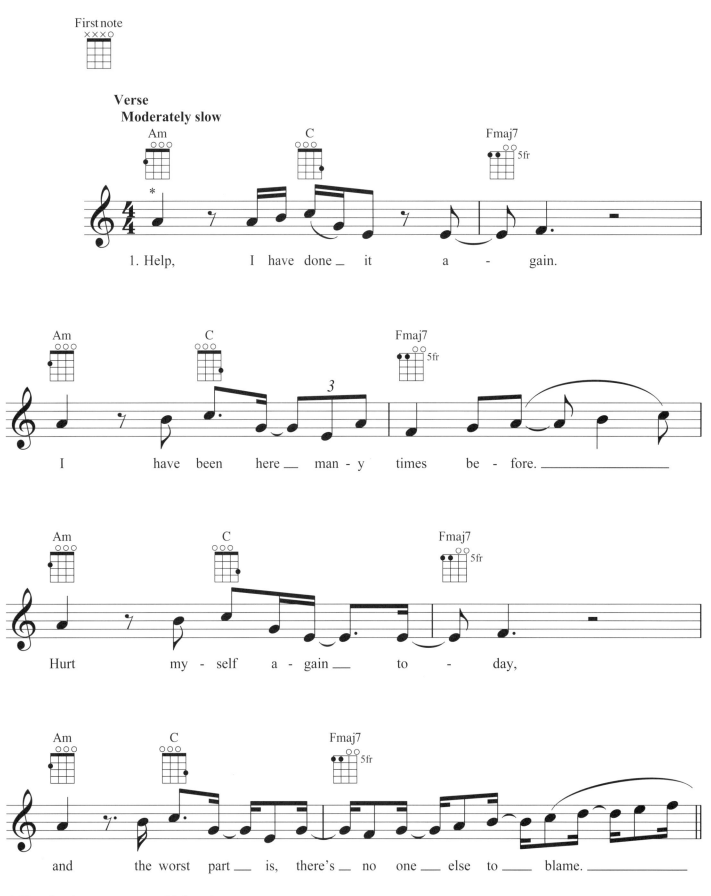

* Vocal written one octave higher than sung.

Copyright © 2004 EMI Music Publishing Ltd. and Complete Music Ltd.
All Rights on behalf of EMI Music Publishing Ltd. Administered in the U.S. and Canada by
Sony/ATV Music Publishing LLC, 424 Church Street, Suite 1200, Nashville, TN 37219
All Rights on behalf of Complete Music Ltd. Administered in the U.S. and Canada by Universal Music - MGB Songs
International Copyright Secured   All Rights Reserved

_____ no - where _____ to _____ be _____ found. Yeah, I think that I _____ might _____

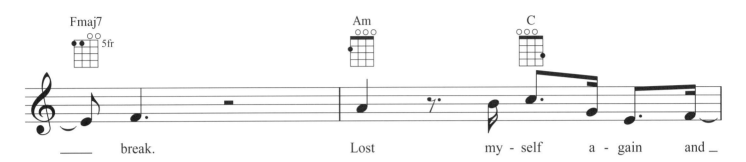

_____ break. Lost my - self a - gain and _____

Chorus

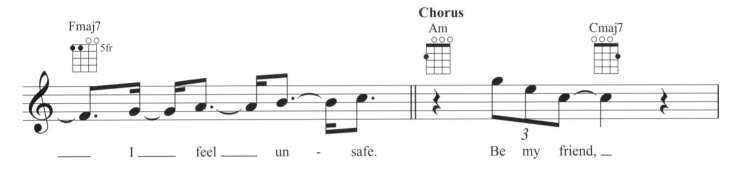

_____ I _____ feel _____ un - safe. Be my friend, _____

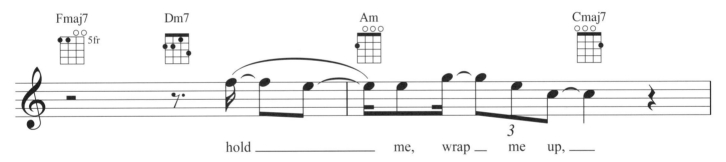

hold _____ me, wrap _____ me up, _____

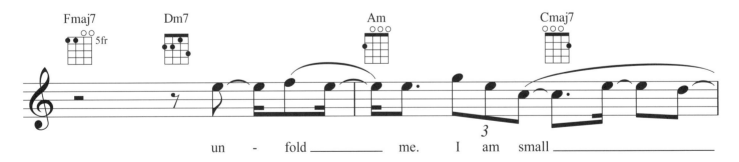

un - fold _____ me. I am small _____

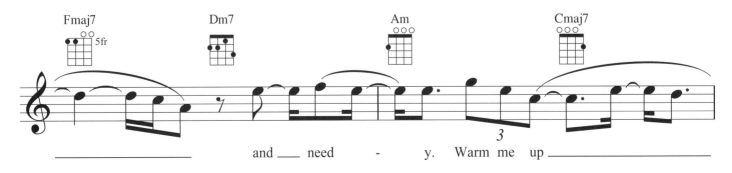

_____ and _____ need - y. Warm me up _____

Chorus

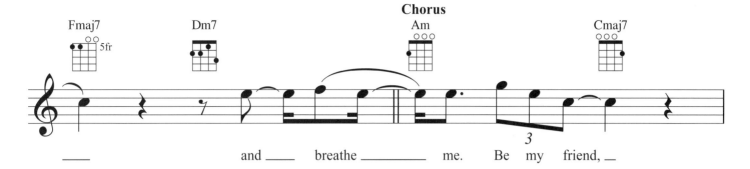

and ___ breathe _____ me. Be my friend, ___

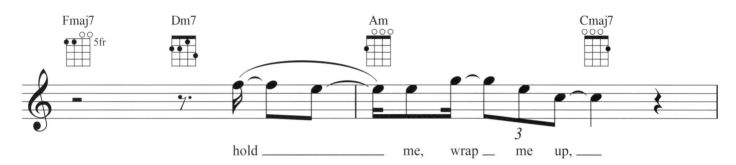

hold _____ me, wrap ___ me up, ___

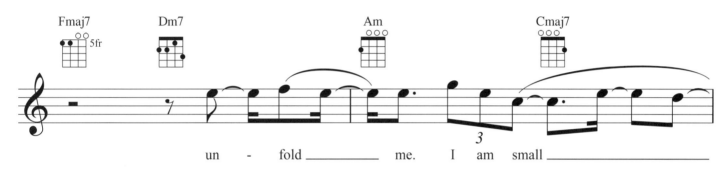

un - fold _____ me. I am small _____

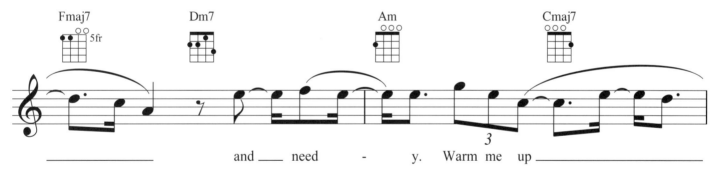

_____ and ___ need - y. Warm me up _____

___ and breathe _____ me.

Outro

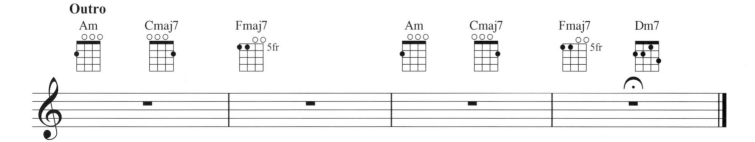

Chasing Cars

Words and Music by Gary Lightbody, Tom Simpson, Paul Wilson, Jonathan Quinn and Nathan Connolly

Copyright © 2006 UNIVERSAL MUSIC PUBLISHING BL LTD.
All Rights in the U.S. and Canada Controlled and Administered by UNIVERSAL - SONGS OF POLYGRAM INTERNATIONAL, INC.
All Rights Reserved   Used by Permission

ev - er was ___ is here in your per - fect ___ eyes,

they're all I can see. I don't know where,

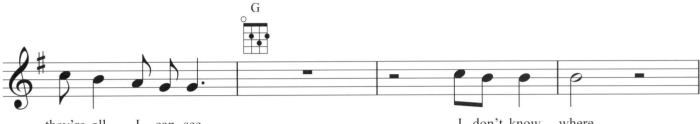

con-fused a - bout how as well. ___ Just know that these

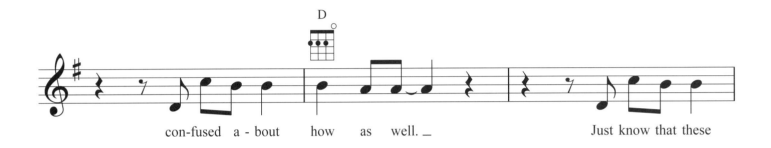

things will nev - er change ___ for us at all. If I lay

Outro-Chorus

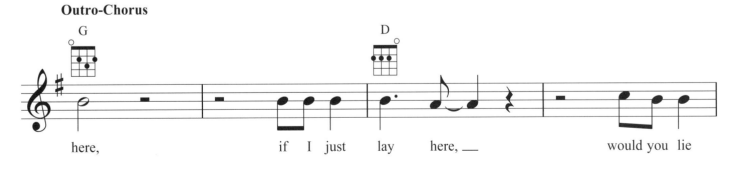

here, if I just lay here, ___ would you lie

with me ___ and just for - get the world?

Come Away with Me

Words and Music by Norah Jones

* *Vocal written one octave higher than sung.*

Copyright © 2002 EMI Blackwood Music Inc. and Muthajones Music LLC
All Rights Administered by Sony/ATV Music Publishing LLC, 424 Church Street, Suite 1200, Nashville, TN 37219
International Copyright Secured   All Rights Reserved

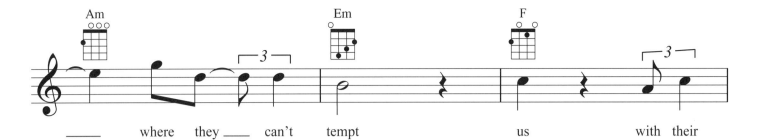

where they ____ can't tempt us with their

Bridge

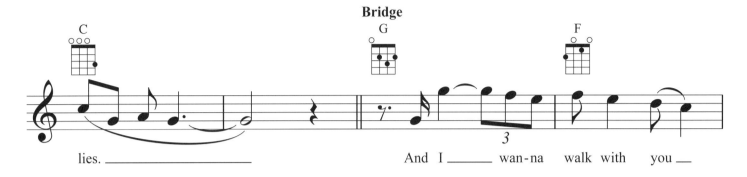

lies. _____ And I ____ wan-na walk with you ___

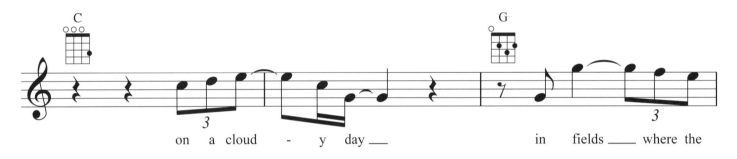

on a cloud - y day ___ in fields ___ where the

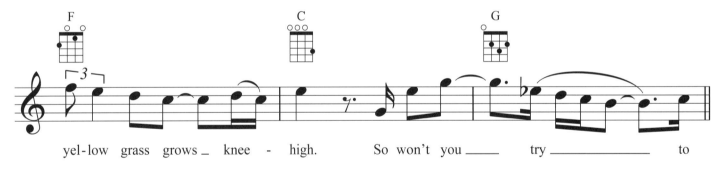

yel-low grass grows_ knee - high. So won't you ___ try _____ to

Verse

3. come? Come a - way ___ with me and ___ we'll kiss on a

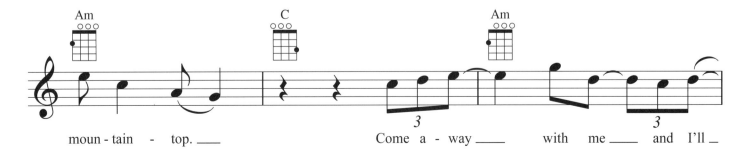

moun-tain - top. ___ Come a - way ___ with me ___ and I'll __

16

never stop lovin' you.

Bridge

And I wanna wake up with the rain fall-

in' on a tin roof while I'm safe there in your arms.

Outro

So all I ask is for you to come away

with me in the night.

Come away with me.

Fix You

Words and Music by Guy Berryman, Jon Buckland, Will Champion and Chris Martin

Copyright © 2005 by Universal Music Publishing MGB Ltd.
All Rights in the United States Administered by Universal Music - MGB Songs
International Copyright Secured   All Rights Reserved

When you love _____ some - one but it goes to waste. ___
But if you nev - er try, you'll ___ nev - er know ___

Could it be worse? _____
just what you're worth. _____

Chorus

Lights will guide _____ you home ___ and ig -

nite _____ your bones, _____ and I will

1.

try _____ to fix you.   3. And high ___

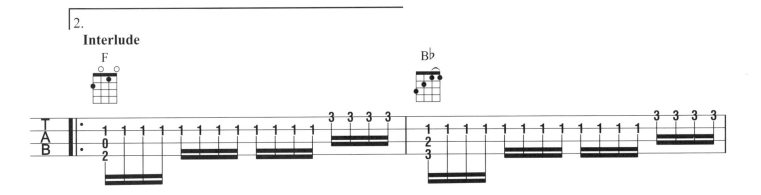

Interlude

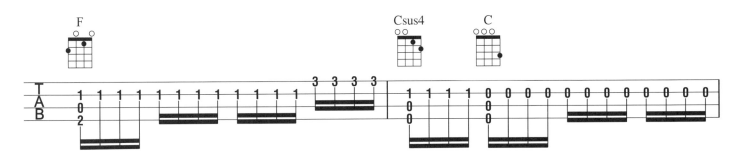

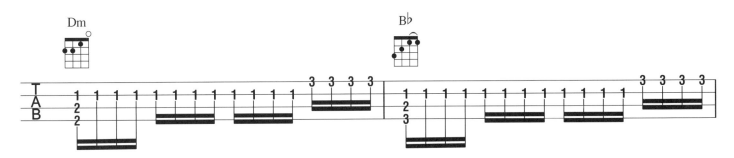

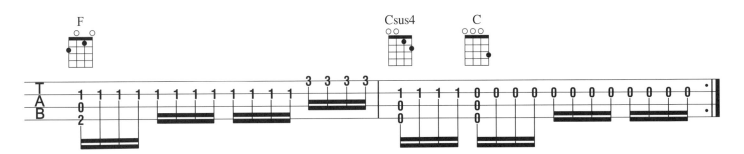

Bridge

Tears stream — down your face — when you lose some - thing

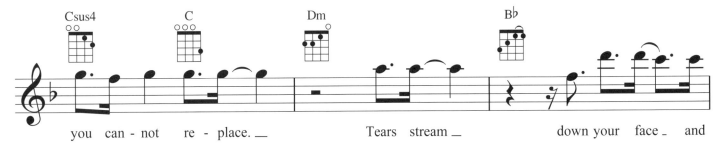

you can - not re - place. — Tears stream — down your face — and

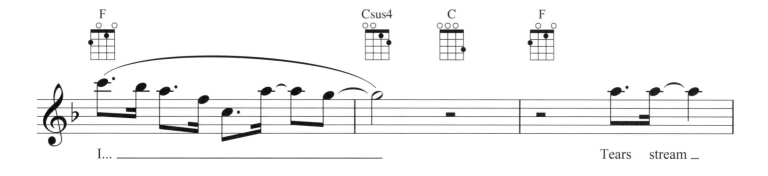

I... _____ Tears stream _

down your face. _ I prom - ise you I ____ will learn from my mis - takes. _

Tears stream _ down your face _ and I... _____

Outro-Chorus

____ Lights will guide _____ you home _

____ and ig - nite _____ your bones, _ and I will

try _____ to fix you. _

Follow the Sun

Words and Music by Xavier Rudd

Copyright © 2012 Sony/ATV Music Publishing (Australia) Pty Limited and EMI Music Publishing Australia Pty Ltd.
All Rights Administered by Sony/ATV Music Publishing LLC, 424 Church Street, Suite 1200, Nashville, TN 37219
International Copyright Secured   All Rights Reserved

re - mem - ber your place. ____ Man - y moons have

ris - en and fall - en long, long be - fore you came. ____ So, which way is the wind ____

____ blow ing, ____ and what does your heart ____

Outro

____ say? So, fol - low, ____

fol - low the sun, _____ and which way the wind

blows when this day is done. ____

Falls

Words and Music by Noonie Bao, Sasha Sloan, Harrison Mills, Clayton Knight and Alexandra Cheatle

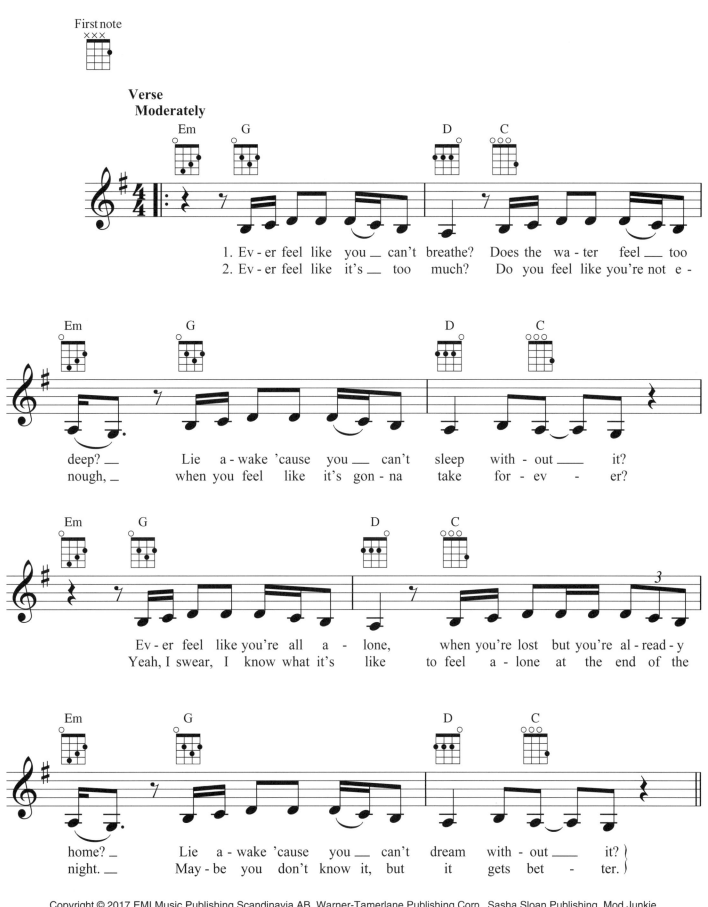

Copyright © 2017 EMI Music Publishing Scandinavia AB, Warner-Tamerlane Publishing Corp., Sasha Sloan Publishing, Mod Junkie, Just Isn't Music Ltd., Harrison Mills Publishing Designee, Clayton Knight Publishing Designee and Songs Of Foreign Family Collective
All Rights on behalf of EMI Music Publishing Scandinavia AB Administered by
Sony/ATV Music Publishing LLC, 424 Church Street, Suite 1200, Nashville, TN 37219
All Rights on behalf of Sasha Sloan Publishing and Mod Junkie Administered by Warner-Tamerlane Publishing Corp.
All Rights on behalf of Just Isn't Music Ltd. Administered by Third Side America
All Rights on behalf of Songs Of Foreign Family Collective Administered by Songs Of Kobalt Music Publishing
International Copyright Secured   All Rights Reserved

Interlude

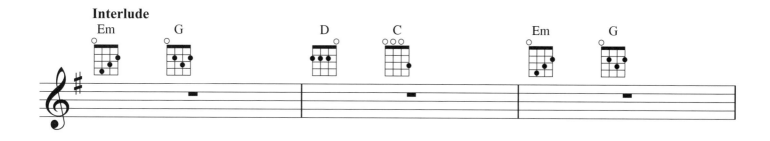

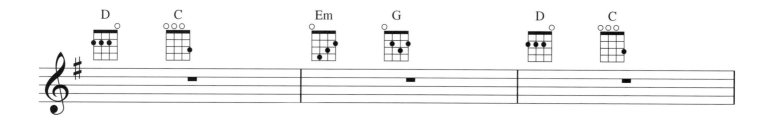

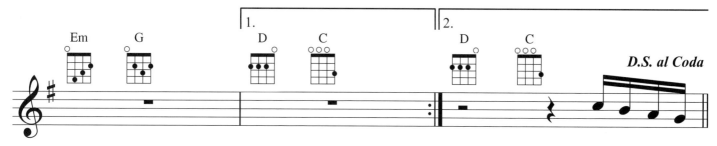

Ev - 'ry - bod - y

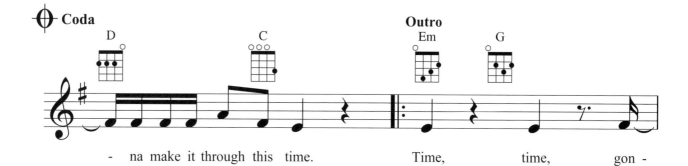

\- na make it through this time.   Time,   time,   gon -

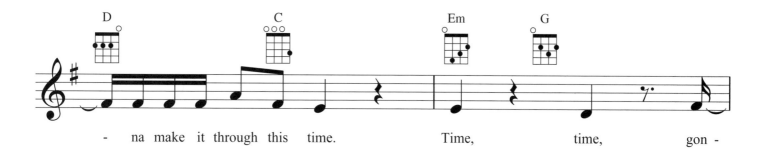

\- na make it through this time.   Time,   time,   gon -

\- na make it through this time.

Heartbeats

Words and Music by Karin Dreijer Andersson and Olof Dreijer

1. One night to be con - fused, one night to speed up truth.
2. One night of mag - ic rush; the start, a sim - ple touch.

We had a prom - ise made, four hands and then a - way.
One night to push and scream, and then re - lief.

Both un - der in - flu - ence, we had di - vine sense
Ten days of per - fect tunes, the col - ors red and blue;

Play 1st time only

to know what to say; mind is a ra - zor blade.
we had a prom - ise made,

Copyright © 2006 BERT'S SONGS LTD.
All Rights in the United States and Canada Controlled and Administered by
UNIVERSAL - POLYGRAM INTERNATIONAL PUBLISHING, INC.
All Rights Reserved   Used by Permission

Ho Hey

Words and Music by Jeremy Fraites and Wesley Schultz

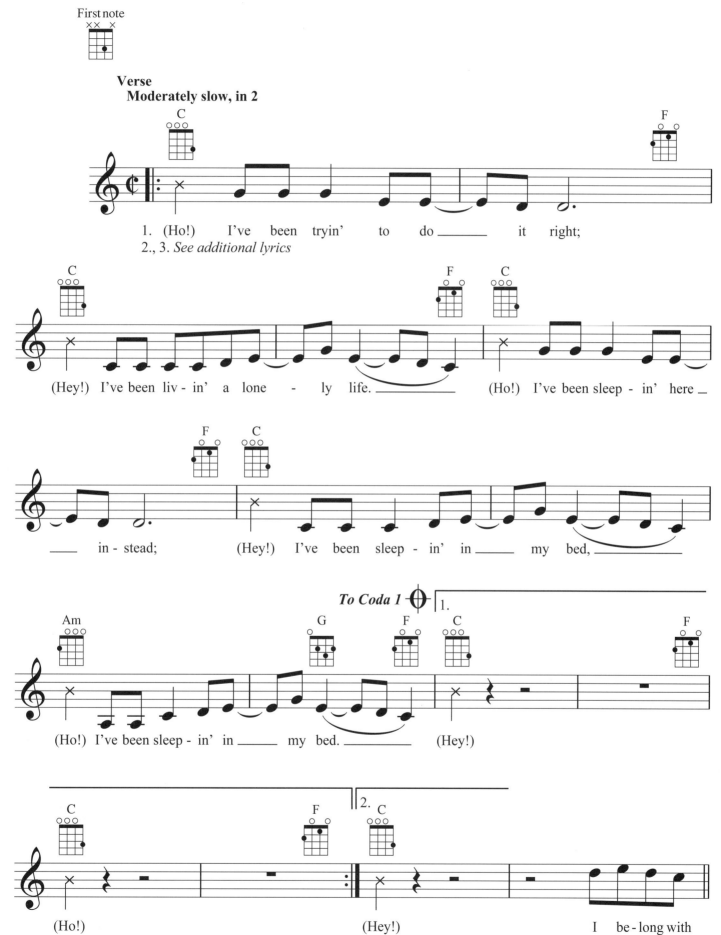

1. (Ho!) I've been tryin' to do _____ it right;
2., 3. *See additional lyrics*

(Hey!) I've been liv-in' a lone - ly life. _____ (Ho!) I've been sleep - in' here _____

_____ in - stead; (Hey!) I've been sleep - in' in _____ my bed, _____

To Coda 1

1.

(Ho!) I've been sleep - in' in _____ my bed. _____ (Hey!)

2.

(Ho!) (Hey!) I be - long with

Copyright © 2011 The Lumineers
All Rights Exclusively Administered by Songs Of Kobalt Music Publishing
All Rights Reserved   Used by Permission

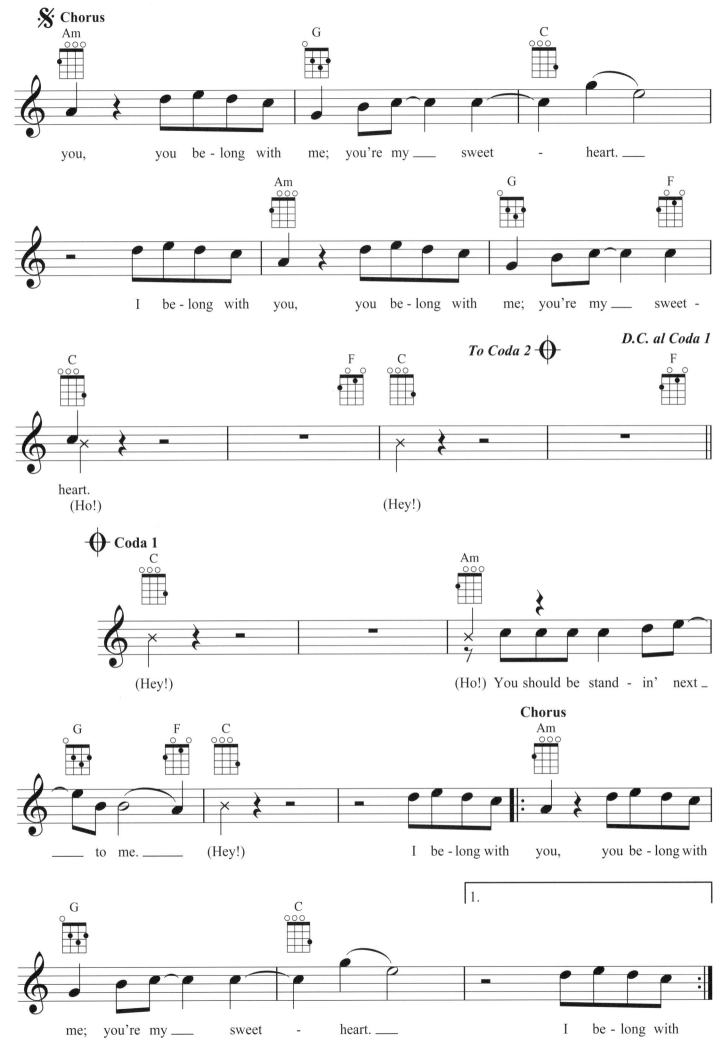

32

Additional Lyrics

2. (Ho!) So show me, family,
   (Hey!) All the blood that I will bleed.
   (Ho!) I don't know where I belong,
   (Hey!) I don't know where I went wrong,
   (Ho!) But I can write a song.
   (Hey!)

3. (Ho!) I don't think you're right for him.
   (Hey!) Look at what it might have been if you
   (Ho!) Took a bus to Chinatown.
   (Hey!) I'd be standing on Canal
   (Ho!) And Bowery. *(To Coda 1)*

Holocene

Words and Music by Justin Vernon

Copyright © 2011 April Base Publishing and Chris In The Morning Music LLC
All Rights Administered by Kobalt Songs Music Publishing
All Rights Reserved   Used by Permission

Coda

C   * C

Let chord ring.

Verse

C

6. Christ - mas night, it clutched the light, __

Am7

the hal - low bright. __

Cmaj7

A -

Cadd9

bove my broth - er, I _____ and tan - gled spines.

C

We smoked the screen __ to make __ it what __ it was __

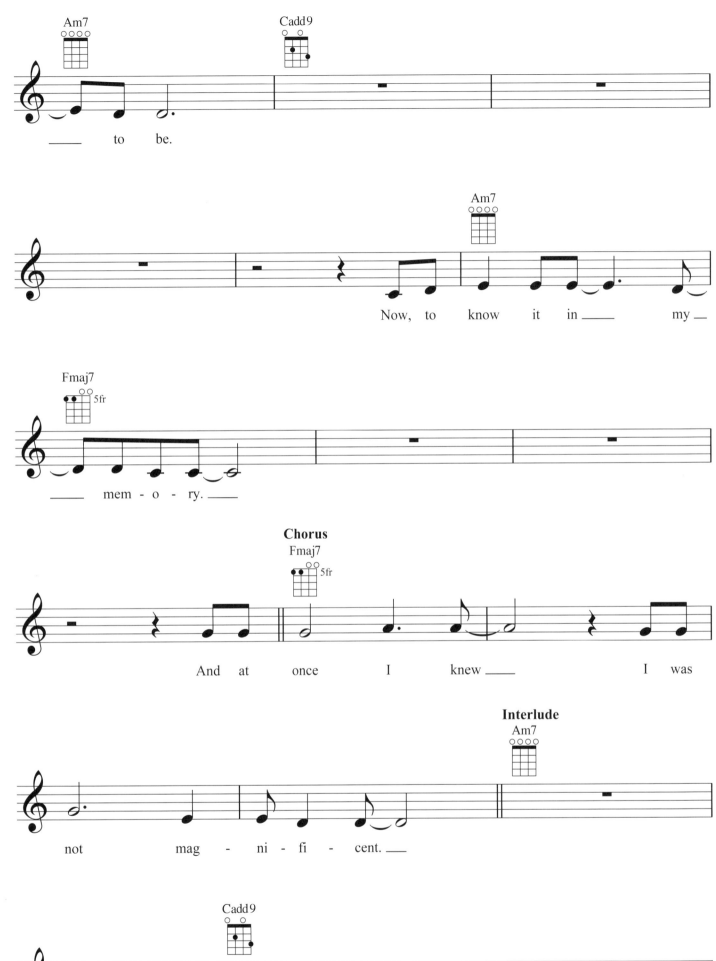

Bridge

High _____ a - bove _____ the high - way _____

_____ aisle.

Jag - ged

va - cance thick with ice _____

and I could see for

miles, miles, _____ miles.

Let Her Go

Words and Music by Michael David Rosenberg

Copyright © 2012 Sony/ATV Music Publishing (UK) Limited
All Rights Administered by Sony/ATV Music Publishing LLC, 424 Church Street, Suite 1200, Nashville, TN 37219
International Copyright Secured   All Rights Reserved

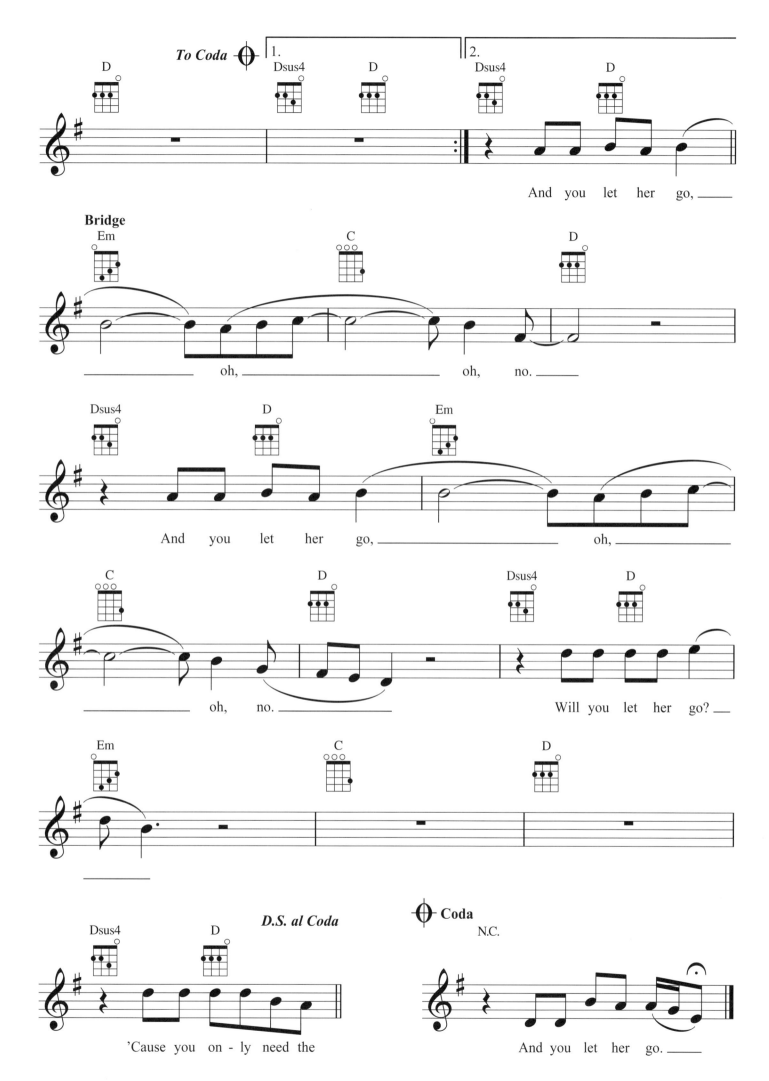

And you let her go, _____

Bridge

_____ oh, _____ oh, no. _____

And you let her go, _____ oh, _____

_____ oh, no. _____ Will you let her go? _____

_____

D.S. al Coda

'Cause you on - ly need the

Coda

And you let her go. _____

Orinoco Flow

Music by Enya
Words by Roma Ryan

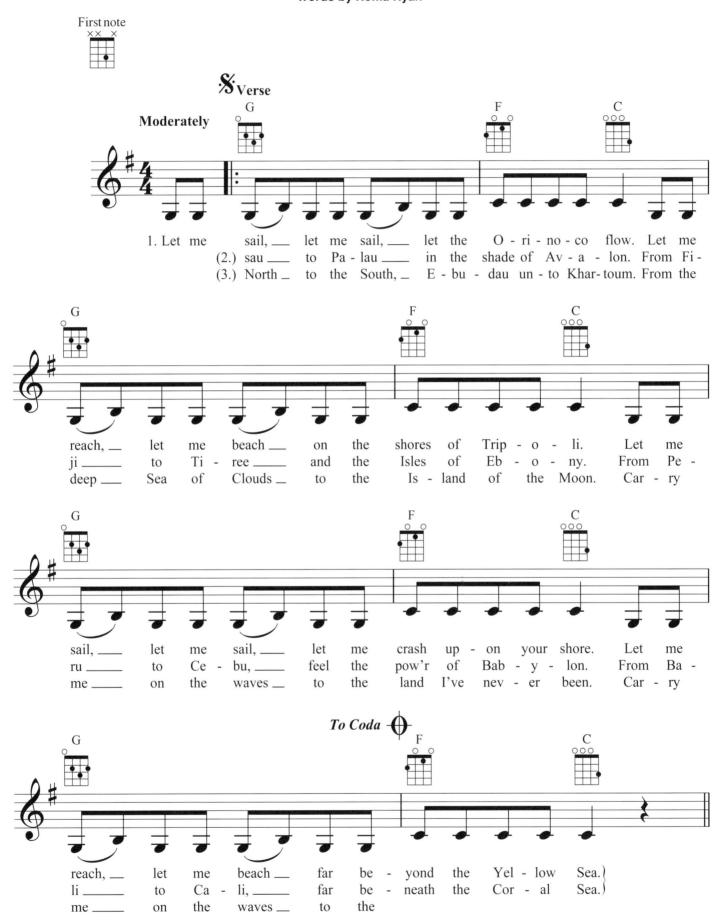

Copyright © 1988 EMI Music Publishing Ltd.
All Rights Administered by Sony/ATV Music Publishing LLC, 424 Church Street, Suite 1200, Nashville, TN 37219
International Copyright Secured   All Rights Reserved

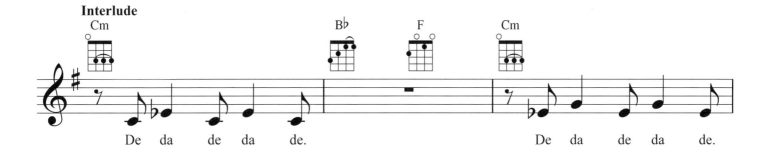

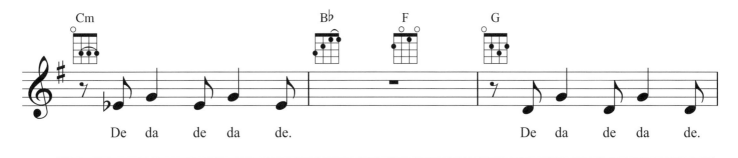

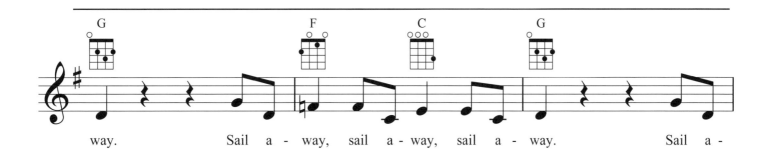

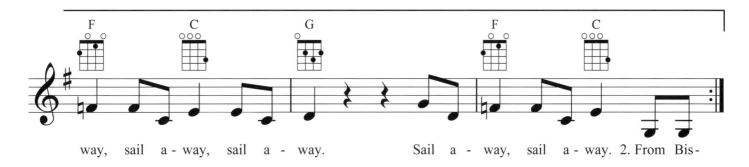

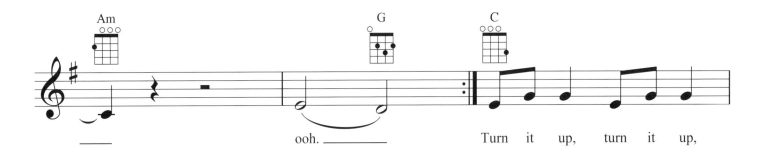

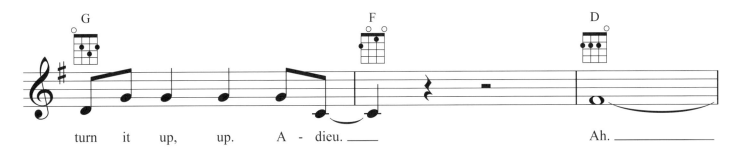

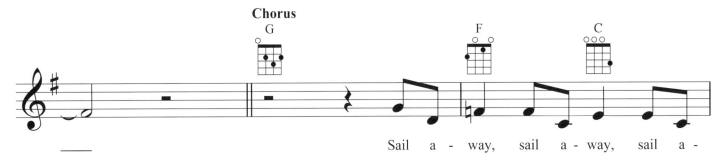

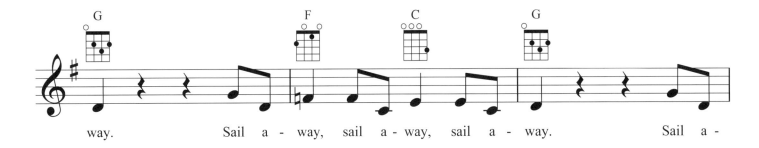

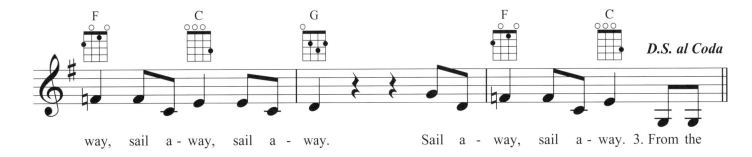

River

Words and Music by Todd Michael Bridges, Chris Vivion, Joshua Block and Austin Jenkins

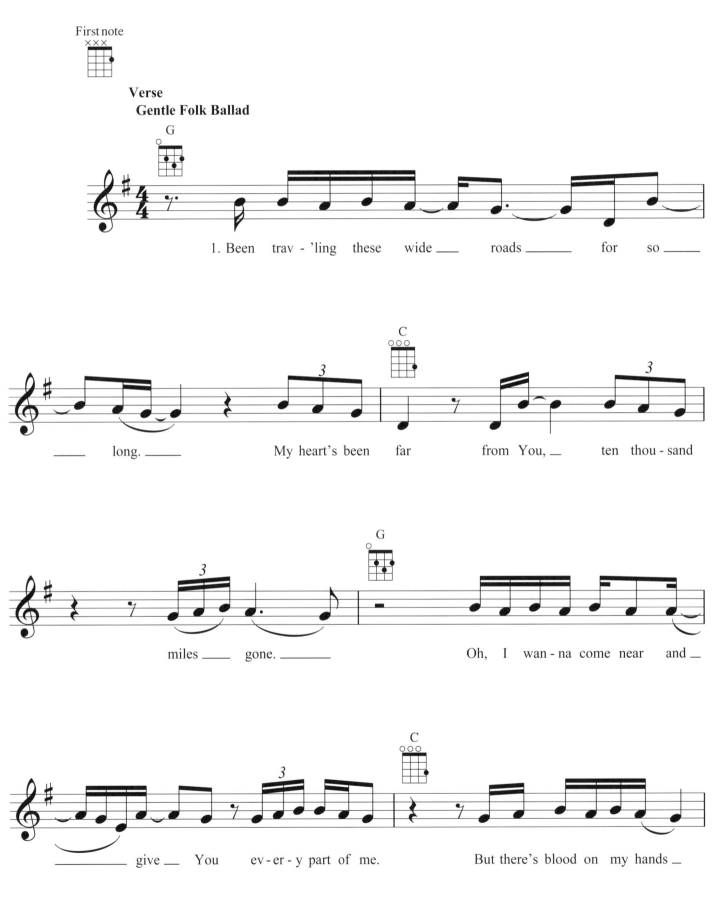

Copyright © 2015 Sony/ATV Music Publishing LLC, EMI April Music Inc.,
Eartha's Gumbo Music, Joshua Block Music, Warneparker and Chris Vivion Music
All Rights on behalf of Sony/ATV Music Publishing LLC, EMI April Music Inc. and Eartha's Gumbo Music Administered by
Sony/ATV Music Publishing LLC, 424 Church Street, Suite 1200, Nashville, TN 37219
All Rights on behalf of Joshua Block Music, Warneparker and Chris Vivion Music Administered by Downtown DLJ Songs
International Copyright Secured   All Rights Reserved

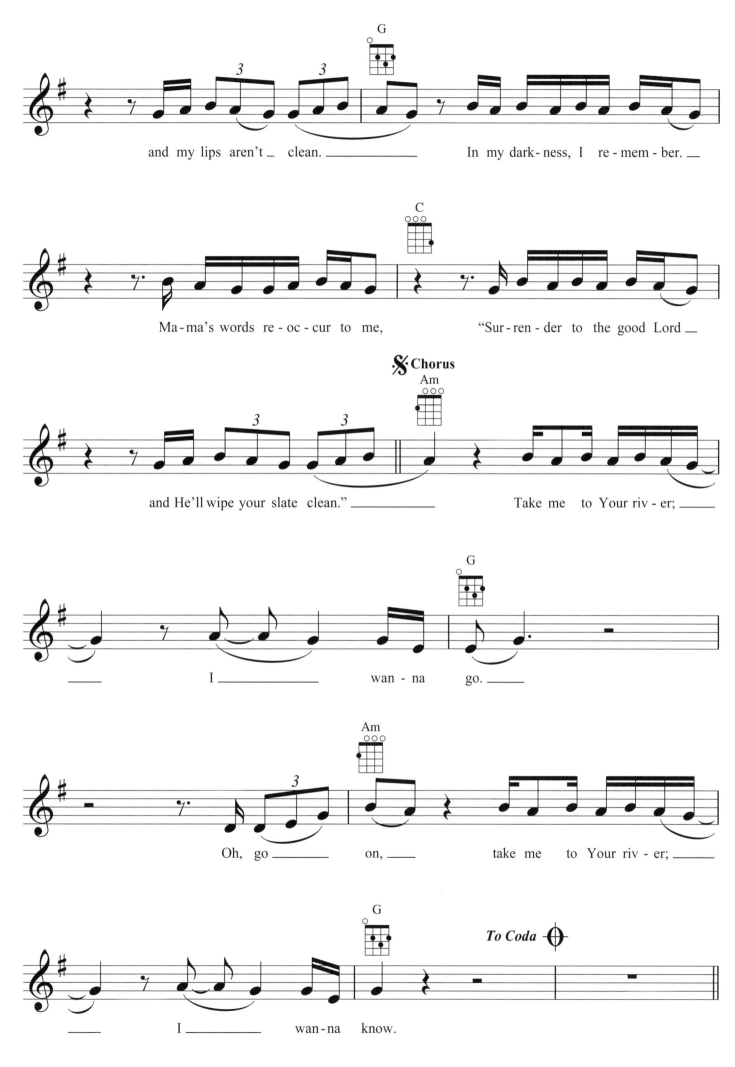

Verse

2. Tip me in Your smooth wa - ters; I _____ go _____ in _____ as a

man with man - y crimes. Come up for air as my sins flow down _____ the

Jor - dan. Oh, I wan - na come near and _____ give _____ You ev - er - y part of me.

D.S. al Coda

But there's blood on my hands _____ and my lips aren't _____ clean. _____

Bridge

Coda

I wan - na go, wan - na go, wan - na go. _____

I wan - na know, wan - na know, wan - na know. _____

Sail Away

Words and Music by David Gray

Copyright © 1999 Chrysalis Music Ltd.
All Rights Administered by BMG Rights Management (US) LLC
All Rights Reserved   Used by Permission

Verse

_____ 1. Cra - zy skies ___ are wild ___ a - bove ___ me now, ___

win - ter howl - ing at my face; _____

and ev - 'ry - thing ___ I held ___ so dear ___

dis - ap - peared ___ with - out a trace. _____

Verse

2. Though all the times ___ I tast - ed love, ___
3. *See additional lyrics*

nev - er knew ___ quite ___ what I had. ___

Additional Lyrics

3. I've been talking drunken gibberish,
   Falling in and out of bars.
   Trying to get some explanation here
   For the way some people are.
   How did it ever come so far?

Sparks

Words and Music by Guy Berryman, Jon Buckland, Will Champion and Chris Martin

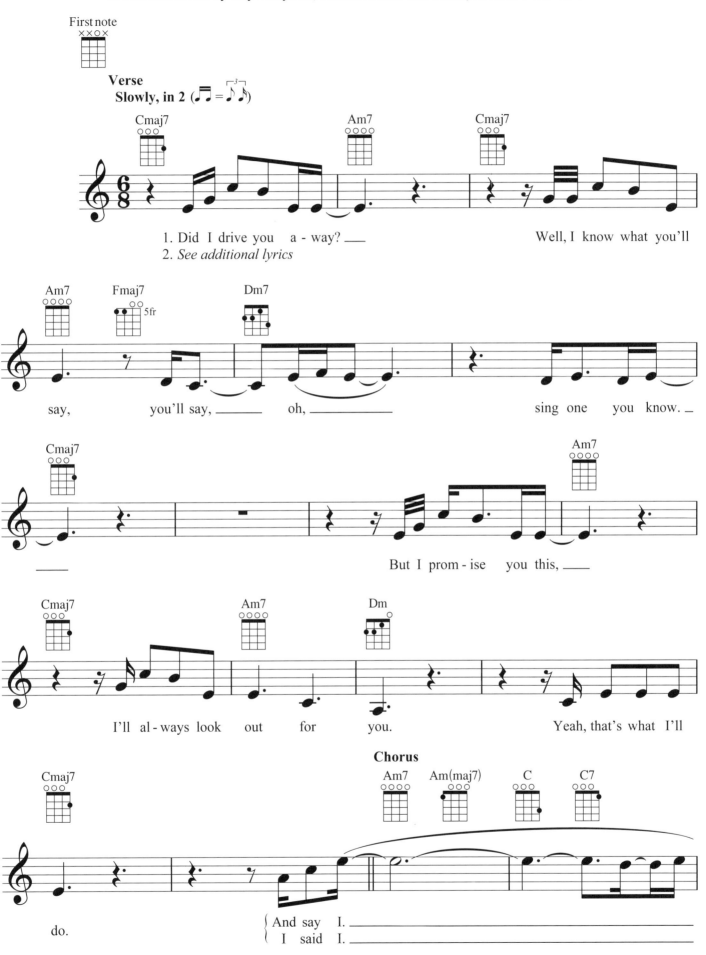

Copyright © 2000 by Universal Music Publishing MGB Ltd.
All Rights in the United States and Canada Administered by Universal Music - MGB Songs
International Copyright Secured   All Rights Reserved

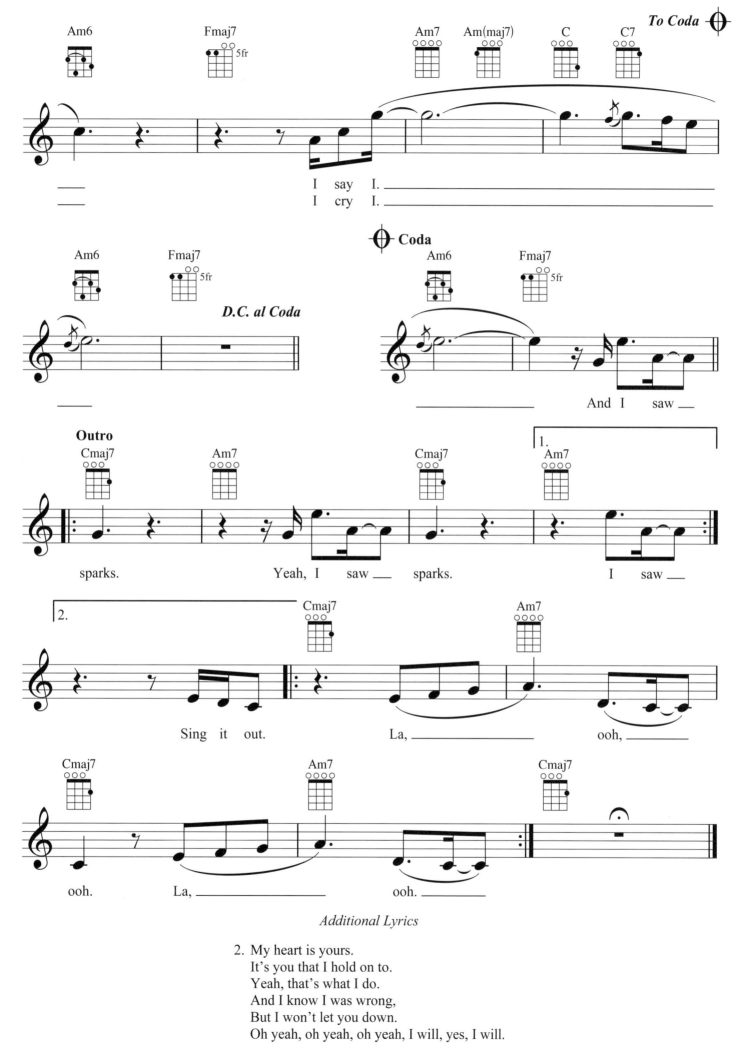

Additional Lyrics

2. My heart is yours.
   It's you that I hold on to.
   Yeah, that's what I do.
   And I know I was wrong,
   But I won't let you down.
   Oh yeah, oh yeah, oh yeah, I will, yes, I will.

Sunrise

Words and Music by Norah Jones and Lee Alexander

Copyright © 2004 EMI Blackwood Music Inc., Muthajones Music LLC and Fumblethumbs Music LLC
All Rights Administered by Sony/ATV Music Publishing LLC, 424 Church Street, Suite 1200, Nashville, TN 37219
International Copyright Secured   All Rights Reserved

Coda

Bridge

Piano solo ends

And now the night ____ will throw its cov - er down, __ ____ mm, on me a - gain. __

Ooh, and if I'm right, __ ____ it's the on - ly way __ to bring me ____ back. _____

Outro-Chorus

Ooh, _____

ooh, _____

ooh, _____   to   you. __

to   you. _____

A Thousand Years

from the Summit Entertainment film THE TWILIGHT SAGA: BREAKING DAWN – PART 1
Words and Music by David Hodges and Christina Perri

Copyright © 2011 EMI Blackwood Music Inc., 12:06 Publishing, Miss Perri Lane Publishing and Warner-Tamerlane Publishing Corp.
All Rights on behalf of EMI Blackwood Music Inc. and 12:06 Publishing Administered by
Sony/ATV Music Publishing LLC, 424 Church Street, Suite 1200, Nashville, TN 37219
All Rights on behalf of Miss Perri Lane Publishing Controlled and Administered by Songs Of Kobalt Music Publishing
International Copyright Secured   All Rights Reserved

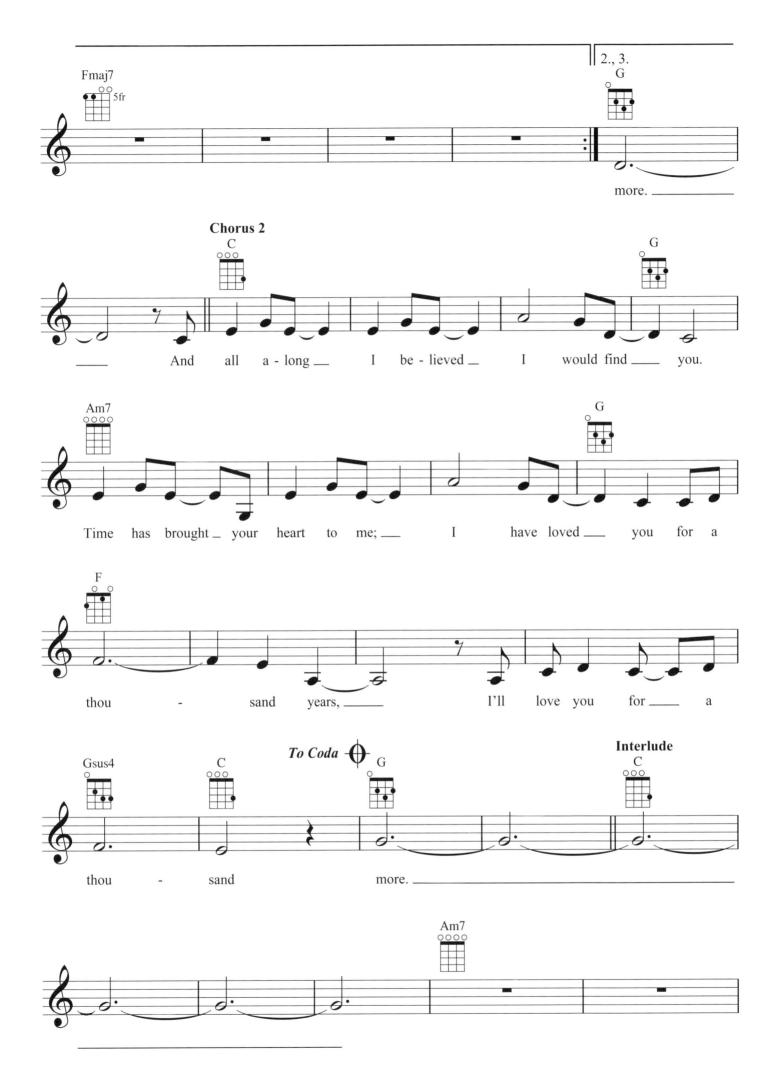

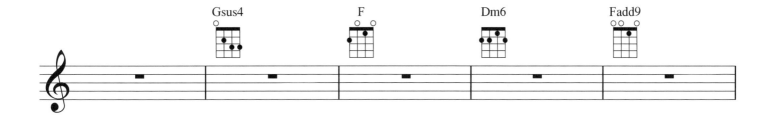

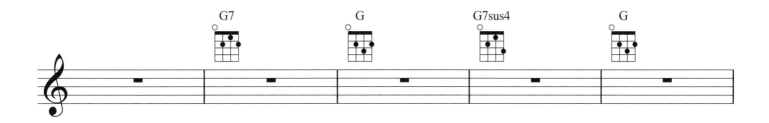

Pre-Chorus

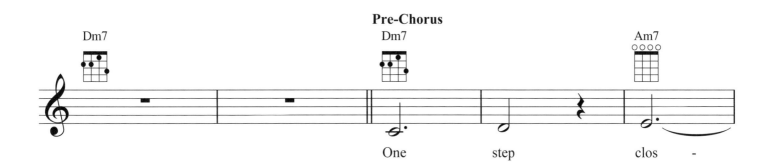

One step clos -

\- er. _____

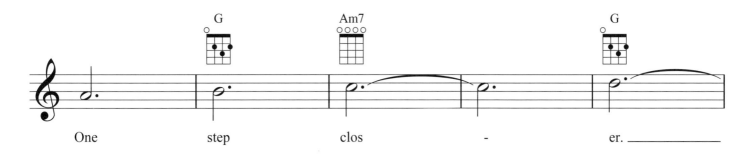

One step clos - er. _____

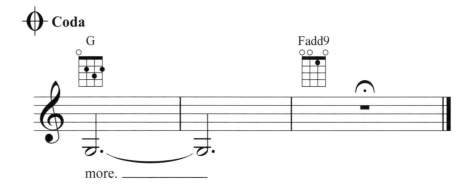

D.S. al Coda
(take 2nd ending)

____

more. _____

Trouble

Words and Music by Ray LaMontagne

Copyright © 2004 BMG Monarch and Sweet Mary Music
All Rights Administered by BMG Rights Management (US) LLC
All Rights Reserved   Used by Permission

Well, I've been _ saved _ by _ a wom - an. I've been _ saved _ by _ a wom - an. I've been _ saved _ by _ a wom - an. She won't let me go. _ She won't let me go _ now. Oh. _

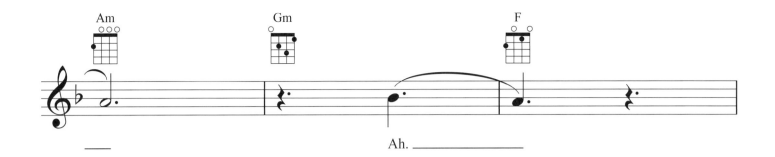

Ah. _____

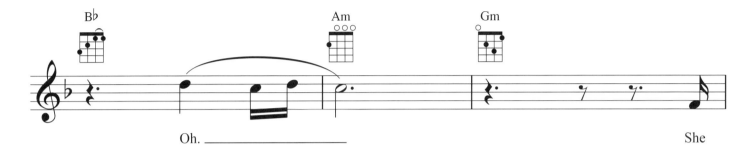

Oh. _____   She

good _____ to me now.   She give me

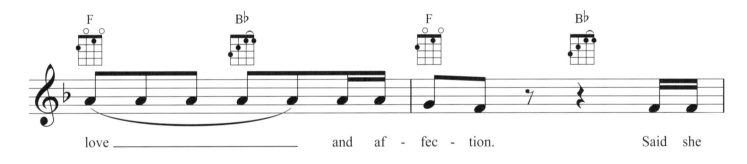

love _____ and af - fec - tion.   Said she

good _____ to me now.   She give me

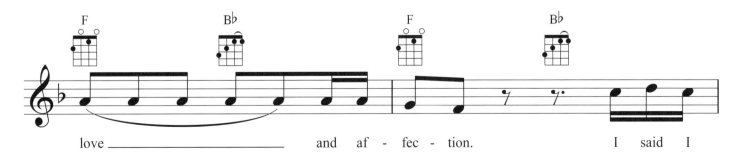

love _____ and af - fec - tion.   I said I

love her.   Yes, I love her.   I said I

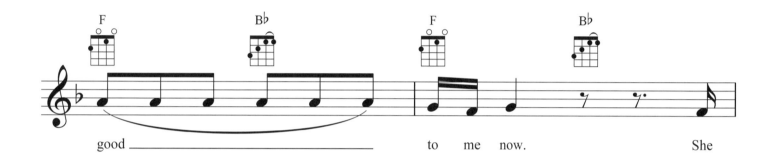

love her.   I said I love... _____   She

good _____ to me now.   She

good   to   me.   She   good   to   me.   Well, I've been ___

D.S. al Coda

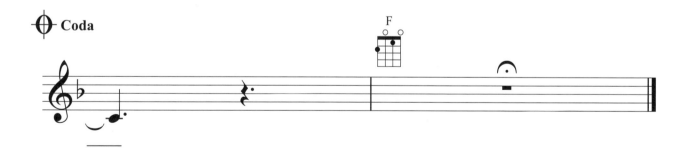

Coda

Additional Lyrics

2. Trouble, trouble, trouble, trouble, trouble.
   Feels like every time I get back on my feet, she come around and knock me down again.
   Worry, worry, worry, worry, worry.
   Sometimes I swear it feels like this worry is my only friend.

I Will Follow You into the Dark

Words and Music by Benjamin Gibbard

Copyright © 2005 BMG Platinum Songs and Where I'm Calling From Music
All Rights Administered by BMG Rights Management (US) LLC
All Rights Reserved   Used by Permission

that they both ___ are sat - is - fied, ___ il -

lu - mi - nate ___ the "no's" ___ on their va - can - cy signs; ___ if

there's no one be - side ___ you when your soul ___ em - barks, ___ then

To Coda ⊕ 1.

I'll fol - low you ___ in - to the dark. 2. In

2. **Verse**

3. You and ___ me ___ have seen ev - 'ry - thing to see, ___

___ from Bang - kok to Cal - ga - ry, and the soles ___ of your shoes ___

Additional Lyrics

2. In Catholic school, as vicious as Roman rule,
I got my knuckles bruised by a lady in black.
I held my tongue as she told me, "Son,
Fear is the heart of love." So I never went back.